To the Little Girl who loved to Dance

Inspirational Poems and Prayers

By Anica L. Walston
Photographs by Charity Brown

Respect the Gender Publishing

Copyright © 2011 Anica Walston
All rights reserved to Author Anica Walston
ISBN: 0983659524
ISBN-13: 9780983659525

Dedication

To

Diamond Coren Brown

February 25, 2000 -February 16, 2011

Contents

Introduction

Part I
Lesson 1

My Prayer
Daily Prayer I
Purpose
Daily Prayer II
At what Cost
Daily Prayer III

Part II
Lesson 2

Disobedience
Daily Prayer IV
Lord's Corner
Daily Prayer V
Dreamer
Daily Prayer VI

Part III
Lesson 3

Paths
Daily Prayer VII
Melanin
Daily Prayer VIII
My last cry
Daily Prayer IX

Part IV
Lesson 4

My eight deadly sins
Daily Prayer X
I heard him say..
Daily Prayer XI
Inspired

Daily Prayer XII

Part V
Lesson 5

3 a.m.
Daily Prayer XIII
Do you know what praise it?
Daily Prayer XIV
I saw heaven
Daily Prayer XV

Part VI
Lesson 6

Restore my family
Daily Prayer XVI
There is doubt
Daily Prayer XVII
If it had not been
Daily Prayer XVIII

Part VII
Lesson 7

Daily Prayer XIX
Does it really matter?
Daily Prayer XX
Beautiful
Daily Prayer XXI

Part VIII
Lesson 8

We can smile together
Daily Prayer XXII
A heavy heart
Daily Prayer XXIII
Respectfully yours
Daily Prayer XXIV

Part IX
Lesson 9
You Decide
Daily Prayer XXV
A breath of fresh air
Daily Prayer XXVI
Make a choice
Daily Prayer XXVII

Part X
Lesson 10
Contract
Daily Prayer XXVIII
How?
Daily Prayer XXIX
Daily Prayer XXX (Evening Prayer)
To the little girl who liked to dance

Epilogue
Acknowledgements
About the Author

Introduction

When I first started my walk with God, I would find myself in settings where the individual leading the prayer would have these elaborate renditions, and offerings of praise. I was jealous because I was a new servant and I wanted what everyone else had. I wanted to freely express my sentiments to God. Then I learned from a good friend that it is not what you say and bellow, but it is, what is in your heart. Therefore, I began to talk to God as if he were my best friend. Through my process, I learned that I had to develop a personal relationship with God.

As my faith increased I found that I could talk to God and be speak freely with my words That is when my thoughts and prayers to God became effortless. They were not elaborate prayers. They were conversations, which I shared with my Lord and Savior. I realized he knew all of me, my thoughts, and how I felt.

As you read these poems, I hope that you are able to relate from your own personal experiences. On my journey, I realized God planted the necessary seeds and touched my heart so that I could be self-aware.

Most of the time we don't even realize how important it is to express. There is value in every expression whether it is positive or negative. It allows us to understand and to put life into perspective. It can teach us to be unbiased and objective. My lessons are just that, my sentiments of daily trials, and triumphs I have had.

I put my thoughts into words and placed them on a canvas to paint a picture. They are small bursts of inspirations that can be vital from day to day. At the end of the day, before we close our eyes we must appreciate the joy of God's wonderful creations. I thank God I was able to embrace my thoughts and share them with all who wish to read.

PART I

Walston

To the Little Girl Who Loved to Dance

Lesson 1

It is morning it is new day. This day has been shaped and carefully molded in the loving arms of God. Make the day a gift. "The gift of obedience." A gift from you to God; for if you are obedient God will surely show you favor. Remember a day is never duplicated so make the best of this day. Start by thinking of ways to please God and execute.

Walston

My Prayer

Dear Lord
Today has not been the greatest day
And my spirit will not allow my tears to fall
from the wells of my eyes

And I was hoping if I envisioned the light
Then it would break cycle of endless stutter and stumble

Lord,
I just don't no sometimes
But I am assured of your glory
Am I supposed to have these feelings?

I should be encourage

So Lord, I don't have much to say
But I will express

That today is hard
And tomorrow will not be duplicated
But if the trial expands in an apparent chaos

Lord
Then I, your servant will just hold on to your glory
I will hold on to your strength

And right now while I write
I will hold onto your word

Daily Prayer I

Oh father the day starts and I often consider not taking on the challenges, concerning myself with the woes and hatred ahead

I do fear
as most men do,
but my fear is only of you

I cannot allow peoples thoughts and behaviors to control me
Even in my minds despair

Sometimes when I pray
My mind often wanders
The turbulence causing a digression in my stream

Lord, I do show weakness and allow my flesh to guide my mind

Which will never work if we are fighting against principalities

Sometime, I appear to smile but there is still sadness in my eyes

That void is the real
that feeling of emptiness sometimes shatters my cognition

And I recognize only you can fill this pit

So I must never act in haste
I dare not ask for strength

To the Little Girl Who Loved to Dance

because I do not wish to face any additional trials

But if it is your will Lord then
It must be done

I will just trust in you so that my day can be counted all joy

I will press through my feelings
And moments that causes
Me to scrape the bottom of sorrow

I will remember to embrace your word
And the positive transmissions from the universe

Even in the day's apparent imperfections
I must witness perfection
For God does all things perfect

So I just pray for guidance and mercy
for the day will not be heavy once it has passed

Father I praise and honor you
for you are the CONSTANT and GREATNESS in my life

Amen

Purpose

It is purpose
it is what makes us whole
we fight, we cry, we live
for the purposes

The purpose that frees us from the evil that tries to tear us apart
our families
our sisters, our brothers, the races, the countries

It is the purpose that wells hatred in our heart
that fights those that are smaller than us
those that can't fight or defend themselves

It is the purpose to believe in idles, science, Buddha, Muhammad, and Jesus Christ
it is what we want to believe in
a purpose

The purpose of man and humanity
The purpose that puts our poor in ghettos
and our ignorant in politics

It is a purpose
it is the obliviousness that we fight every day
and hope that we win
even if we don't have a chance

It is a purpose
That makes me calm, angry, bitter, and happy
at the same time

It is my purpose to journey on, and face the trials
that God has lain before me
It should be our purpose to live in one accord
in perfect harmony

But is our purpose to continue to deny
that without his blessings
It would not be possible to have a purpose
It is our purpose
It is our fight
It is our deliverance and justification
It is what we love
Who we love
Where we love
It what we need to have purpose

Daily Prayer II

Dear father last night
I went to bed with a song of rejoice in my heart
and it lingered in my spirit

Until you blessed me to open my eyes
and smell the rays
from the sunshine

I want to say thank you
because there are days when I feel that
there is no congruence

I feel like the wrong key was struck
and it bound my spirit into a lapse

Father forgive me because I sometimes forget
that your hands touch everything that moves and
breaths

So that I may realize
The trial, is but my test
to remember my faith

And when I forget
That you are guiding me through temptation
The devil will attempt to fill me with shame
and because of your righteousness in me

I know that, it is not of you

For you are merciful
and you greet me in my good and bad

You console the emptiness
that seems like and abyss of emotions
that hide in my subconscious

You are my beginning
My knight in shining armor
My prince on a white horse
You are the omnipotence in my life

Even in my saturation of the mundane
you still uphold me

My push to thrive
My push to righteousness
My moment of salvation

Lord I thank you for the daily revelation

And promises kept
For you are a God of his word
And your word lives in me

Amen

At what Cost

I look in the mirror and realize

That I see

The hurt, guilt, and shame

I see that my color has turned from a golden sunray to a gray prison wall

My finances dwindled, because I hold the security in the domicile

I am frustrated trying to figure out when we switched roles

Am I a man?

Am I the provider?

Clearly, I didn't read your word, to understand my place in Gods kingdom

Clearly, I made decisions without Gods counsel

But I was in love

In love

What is in love?

Cause according to me it is okay for someone to beat you down mentally and spiritually

It is ok for me to work like a dog and supply everyone's need

Clearly, I am hypocrite

I know better

I know what I wanted

And I am aware of my expectations

They are all clearly outlined in a resume for those seeking employment

But I didn't screen the applications

I settled
Thank you Satan
For reminding me the cost of ignoring God

Daily Prayer III

Today father
I pray for clarity

To the Little Girl Who Loved to Dance

Validity
Spirituality
and a
Mature mentality

A step ahead of those who wish to be lost

Even in your freedom of will
Father I choose you

For I don't know perfection like you
I don't understand mercy, as you hand it out

But I watch those that are ignorant
Blaspheming; energy from their poor cognitive processes

I do humble myself, for at times, I know not what I do
In consciousness my awareness becomes minimal

I have allowed my flesh

To hold my peace captive

So I look to the heavens for those guiding lights

Clarity in that, I know which direction

Validity, in the truth of my father's promises
Spirituality, as my father runs through my soul

And the mentality to uphold his words!
Thank you
Father
Amen

Walston

To the Little Girl Who Loved to Dance

Part II

Walston

Lesson 2

So when you are trapped don't look for the exit, close your eyes, fall to your knees, and allow his mercy, to start operating on your soul.

Walston

Disobedience

I will not scream because you refuse to listen when I spoke

I will no longer cry because you have hurt my feelings

I will no longer fear because you have threatened my life

I will no longer be in rage because you don't appreciate the calm

I will no longer run because you can't catch me

I will no longer apologize because you have beaten me senseless

I will no longer be aroused because you have an erection

I will no longer refute love because you don't love me

I will no longer surrender to alcohol and pills because you have made me nervous

I will no longer be indecisive because you made all the decisions

I will no longer be restless because you didn't allow me to sleep

I will no longer be interrupted because you didn't want me to pray

I will no longer surrender my soul because someone told you, you were God

I will no longer be selfish because you refuse to share

I will no longer neglect my child because you want my attention

I will no longer be afraid of being a woman because you chose not to be a man

And I will not look back because I refuse to turn to salt

Daily prayer IV

Today Lord
I wish you to bless my tongue
for at times my words
do not always, reflect the positive images of life

I have a habit of discounting my fruitfulness

Lord

By not being, aware of the power of expression

Even when I speak casually,
I should be conscious at all times
So that I am not leaving the devil an open door

Lord I cannot allow him a pass at the gate
Because I didn't chase my tongue

To the Little Girl Who Loved to Dance

In my conversation Lord tame my spirit
So that when I speak
I speak love and life into existence

Lord tame my spirit, so when I breathe
I breathe life into the newly planted seeds of success

Lord when I cry, replenish my soul from the woes
and cares of the day

Lord in my confusion, speak equilibrium into
consciousness

For Lord I know from your words
And with them, I fill my cup
so that I am overflowed

If I submit to your words then my anointing will
expand

So that I may share a captivating life with all your
wonderful creations

So that I may lead by example
For these things are promised by you

So Lord with a tongue that is used wisely
Can be respected
and embraced

For I am able to use words that will
impact those in a positive realm
That too wish to be enthralled in your grace

Amen

Lord's Corner

When the bills arrive and the how is unknown just stop and take a deep breathe
There's no time to allow the devil in your sight cause it could cause you to be careless

When the cabinets are almost bare, anxiety ignites, and your stomach begins to rumble
Bend on one knee, shout some praise, smile, and become eternally humble

When the love and security is gone, you feel empty and want to claim defeat
Remember you words, lessons learned, and fall directly at his feet

Favor will be shown by a merciful man who will never be a foreigner
Just remember to take your burdens to the Lord and leave them in the Lord's Corner

Daily Prayer V

I smile
As the day begins
My new beginnings of life

I smell roses and my heart will whimper at the site
Of his wonderful name
I am empowered to move closer to his path
of righteousness

To the Little Girl Who Loved to Dance

My soul is hoping to fill my cup
with a rejuvenation of his spirit.

I am elated with the opposition for I will see my
father's works manifest into glory

Only as my day begins
can I evaluate to the sweet birth of the intangibles and
tangible
New beginnings

I feed off of his proposition of pearly gates and
faraway places that overflow with the sweet nectar of
the land

It is my peace that makes the day glorious
It is my carefree heart that sings his song

Lord what wonder
oh what grace

And for this, I am thankful to open my eyes
and employ your beauty

Thank you father
As my day begins

Dreamer

I dreamed of wealth, prosperity, beauty, and faith
I dreamed of sacrifices, hope, love, and fate

I dreamed of giants and natures frolicking fruits
I dreamed of times spent together in my youth

I dreamed of love lost, loved gain and the love that I still seek
I dreamed of happiness and strength for the strong and meek

I looked toward God to complete me and keep me still
I dreamed a dream and prayed it was real

Daily Prayer VI

So today father
I am full of emotion
That I don't understand

I pray to you
for I need an ease
I know where these feelings stem from
I just don't know why they are here

I pride myself on delighting in my control of falling on your word
But today Lord there is a disruption in my spirit
It is a feeling of loss

To the Little Girl Who Loved to Dance

It is a feeling of missing something that use to be tangible
It is a feeling of separation
It is a feeling of unwanted isolation

I just want to belt out and scream at the heavens and shake hell
For I feel
Like I am overwhelmed with sentiments of tarnished remembrance

Things that did not benefit my spirit
And I still held them close
Lord please take me back to my feelings of calmness

Please rejuvenate your power
For I feel like a child lost in a place
Of woe

I cannot maintain this feeling for surely I will die
I need you to breathe life back into my thoughts
Dissipate the feeling of sorrow

Restore me Lord
For I no longer
want to feel the anxiety of lost

Walston

To the Little Girl Who Loved to Dance

Part III

Walston

Lesson 3

If everything seems to be moving at a slow pace, do not hit the fast forward button, be patient. Trust that God is working. Continue to prayer and stay faithful. As long as you are obedient and are productive, God is always moving at his pace even if you get antsy and want to move faster.

Walston

Paths

If I were not able to taste the cool of an ice cube
I would not know what it is to have tasted the snow

If I were not courageous
I would not know what it is to have fear

If I were not impatient
I would not know what it is to be humbled

If I were not indignant
I would not know what it to find euphoria

If I did not fast
I would not know what it was to be hungry

If I did not lie
I would not understand the importance of truth

If I did not cry
I would not know what it is meant to purified

If I did not run
I would not know what it means to stand still

If I did not submit
I would not have the opportunity to find glory

If I did not die
I would not know what it is to be born again

If I did not sing
I would not know what it is meant to be heard
If I did not write then

I would not understand what it is meant to be relevant

If I did not seek God
I would still be trying to understand…

Why am I lost?

Daily Prayer VII

Lord I here silence
I don't hear weeping or whining
Laughter or praise

Lord I just here silence
For my mind is clear
Ready to absorb
New pieces of life

The silence reminds me to think
And process

The silence allows me to remember
The alone

The silence allows me to only call out your name
In a moment of despair.

Lord I am only a child
Wrapped in your loving arms
Trying to understand where I am and what I will be

I feel full of fear
But I am fearless

I feel unwanted
But I am aware of loves presence

I am not sure what I conjures in the day
That leaves my most personal trials
To weigh heavy

Lord I will not fret
For my wandering eye will lead me in the direction of comfort in your arms

Melanin

It illuminates off of my brown hue
with distinguished tones of accented oranges and olive green

It shows the ripples in my eyes
Defining my pupils and retina, which allow me sight

My heart ticks and murmurs
as the blood rushes through my veins to sustain existence

And my brain begins to categorize and calculate a plan
I feel the rays stretch across my temple filling me with

The energy that is needed for my survival
I dare not doubt my power for I am in existence because of its non-extinction

I am the elite,
which those that lack pigment, all dream to be

from the kink in my locks to the thickness in my lips
and the shadow of my hips

I am not just any creature
I am a child of the sun

Daily Prayer VIII

Heavenly father,
I come to you as your humbled servant

I am asking
God for you

To show me what seat of responsibilities
will I hold
Here on earth

For father I
Want to honor you
And spread favor
As you have given me favor

Lord I request a double
Portion

A portion, which will enrich my soul in glory
A portion that will allow me to experience
Your Holy Spirit

For father I want to be fed
I want you to swell my
Belly
With hope

I want to shout tears of joy
As I incline my brothers and sisters
To engage in your beauty

Lord just tell me and I
Will obey
Lord command me
for I
Fall at your knees

Lord order my steps
Organize my thoughts
Hand me my mission Lord

And watch the fire ignite in my spirit
As I witness to the world your greatness

Whatever you want me to do
For my faith and works will increase
Just by your command
Amen

My last cry

See I cried my last tear yesterday
When the storm came
And the wind blew turbulence in my life
When my pockets were empty

Along with the gas tank
And my heart

When everything failed
Friends left and disappointed
Trust were tarnished
And lies escaped the mouth
Of my enemies
To harm me

You see I cried my last tear yesterday

When her body was lifeless
And she could no longer tell me
She loved me
When my innocence was removed
And sin befriended me

When hope turned to shame
Guilt turned to pain
And nowhere surrounded me
While loneliness held me captive

You see I cried and I cried

Because I saw, nothing and visions were unclear
And the mountains were too high to climb
My feet stood still
While my flesh was on fire
And nothing or no man
Came to my rescue
I cried

Then he grabbed tears
And heard my plea

To the Little Girl Who Loved to Dance

He asked me a question
And I received
For there was nothing else for me to do
And I wanted and yearned timeless peace

He sent an angel down
And he covered me
He spoke to me through kindness and his gentleness
touched my heart
And my spirit was set free
And my battles changed hands

He promised
And he honored his word
That is my life today and every day thereafter
Cause I made up my mind
That the Lord was mine
And weeping only came in my night
And now there is joy during my morning time

So when life is a trifle
And trouble follows you
And the tears well your eyes
And you don't know what to do

Call on his name claim
And receive
Believe in his word
He will never leave
And will never stray
See that is why
I cried my last tear yesterday

Daily Prayer IX

Lord,
I bow my head and I glance at two of your great creations
the power they hold, the strength they can build
for these tools are what carry me through the day

For me they guarantee, that your works can be completed to your liking
God I do understand that everyone does not own these treasures
and I know how precious they are
They give me an extension of security
and they hold each heart they touch

God I praise your name
For without them I could not write
I give thanks
I am forever humbled and
and grateful
for my hands

Amen

Part IV

Walston

Lesson 4

Being a parent is than barking orders and spoiling them rotten. Your children are little replicas of you. They have feelings; they suffer thru trials and strife.

They have something to say, questions to be answered. We must be diligent as parents and listen. Make them feel comfortable enough to share. For you do not want them two learn their morals and values from negative entities. They should learn from you. So listen to them. You will realize they have something to say.

My eight deadly sins

So in anger
I cuss, scream, shout, damn, and plot

With happiness
I smile, pretend, and hope for a favorable outcome

With anxiety
I shake, can't breathe, and become dizzy

In sorrow
I cry, feel distant, depressed, and create the ultimate isolation

In greed
I become self-centered, self-righteous, and petty

In organization
I become anal, focused, meticulous, and obsessive

In lust
I become submissive, promiscuous, and crave with an insatiable appetite

And in love
I hold patience, grace, and the unconditional expectations never reciprocated

Daily Prayer X

Dear Lord,
I pray for those today who have put their trust in man

Listening to the ins and outs of ugly

that happens on our porches and in back yards daily

The ignorance that lurks in our hallways and street corners

Entrapment in a mental slavery of impoverishment

Lord, those that listen to the media as they interpret the chaos of the land

Those that fear the recession

Those that are losing their material treasures and going into a state of panic

Those losing the real purpose and understanding of their lives

Those lacking education and expanding knowledge

Those that lack comprehension of what they encounter daily

Lord for it is all in your hands

We are passengers on your train
You are our conductor

To the Little Girl Who Loved to Dance

Once we understand your position

then and only then will we understand that the country is in a recession,

the stupid do not wish to find truth,

the ignorant do not seek a betterment

But those that are under his anointing, and believe in their Lord and Savior Jesus Christ
are not

for his promises hold truth

His words list abundance and favor

Not tragedy and despair

Only trials, and tribulations that he orchestrates for lessons learned

And Lord I dare not doubt you

We need to understand that if we don't increase our knowledge in your work

If we don't pray for an increase in our faith

than we will be lost in a time zone that will
Ends in the shadows of hell
Lord I fear this place for I want to be close to you

I want my children to be close to me

So that we can gaze in your glory

So that we can gaze at salvation

For it is the fruit of this land and eternities

Let us recognize and honor our master

Let us trust and understand as he steers us into his promises

We will never be forsaken

Lord I trust in your words

I believe in your promises

Amen

I heard him say...

I heard him say let us go into the house
For he is what I hear when the sun light hits my face
It is the song that plays in my head as I sleep and converse with the angels in my dreams

I heard him say let us seek him out
For the understanding and wisdom he possesses
Cause we are made is his image, and his grace is upon us

I heard him say to wait patiently and trust
For he has never forsaken and he honors his word

And as I humble myself, the Lord hears my plea in my time of trouble
And supplies all my needs

I heard him say that he anoints my head with oil
For he covers me with his blood for he is the lamb
The almighty Lamb of God
There is no other that can be called by his name

I heard him say ask, and it shall be given
Seek, and ye shall find
For my faith will never waiver, and expectancy is the stance I will hold
And be still and know he is God

I heard him say come to me with boldness
Fear no man but me
And declare sweet victory
For when I claimed my Jesus
He set my soul free!

Daily Prayer XI

Lord today
I am forever grateful for influence
And the lessons learned
The power to sway

The power that somebody has to affect other people's thinking or actions by means of argument,

Example or force of personality

Influences that cause us to forget about the truth in your word

Influences that allow us to include innovations that have no place in your kingdom

The influences that hold no positive justice in the choices we make

We are fools

With will

The will that you freely gave us to try to make better judgments

I would love to just be wrapped in your influence

I would love not to be drawn nearer to the
unfurnished promises of Satan
But clearly Lord, I am weak
So I stretch my hand to the heavens with the hopes

Of touching the hem of your garment

That will restore

Discipline and obedience

For God when I am influenced

I do not lean to your right hand

I bow at temptation

To the Little Girl Who Loved to Dance

And I know this does not please you

So please empty

The treachery from my spirit

So I will not carry the spirit of trepidation

I want to follow and carry your word close to my heart

So Lord, I ask for help and the reduction

Of the influence that does not satisfy

My father

Inspired

So I am inspired by waterfalls, cool breezes,
Love, autumn, thunderstorms
Hurricanes and soft music
The sounds of a baby crying, and the stroke of a clock trying to beat a deadline

Dogs barking, cars stopping, inspire me,
Traffic jams of the unnecessary
Winds that blow just the treetops
A flowers scent that leaves a mystic melody in my thoughts

I am inspired by people laughing, tragedy, the rise and fall of a nation that is fatherless

but its mother has the strength to endure the tests of time
Birds chirping a cry for peace
And hints of why, what if, and those that dare to dream

Yes, I am inspired
By a pencil, that shades paper
With colorful metaphors, and crystal verbiage
That describes the essence of beauty around

The warmth of a good man, and the rejection from a weak one releasing me to the betterment of my existence

Yes, I am inspired
By chaos, calamity, organization, and omnipotence
The greatness in which we all wish to achieve

The majestic majesty of natural wonders that comfort the earth
And allow me to know that I am human and humane

Yes, I am inspired
By a God who has surrendered his son in the name of our sins, and will not forsake even when I am wretched and undone
Allows me to repent, and cleanse myself in his fiery words
and seek knowledge until I see my salvation

Yes, I am inspired
And free because I dare to be just me
For I am covered and hidden in the Secret place of the Almighty

Never to question my faith, hope, talents and hearts desires

Yes, I am inspired

Daily Prayer XII

Good day Lord,

I could if I wanted,

To start singing the praises to the heavens

I could shout, and scream about the goodness & mercy of God
I could run through the streets with your word in my hand
I could bless a lost soul with your love and kindness

I could call a friend and listen to the joys, and woes of their day

I could kiss my children a hundred times, and admire nature's wonders

I could feed the homeless, and counsel the strays

I could dance like David, and have hundreds fall to my feet

I could go on and on trying to figure out how to pray

Including empty quotations that have not been sown into my soul

But God today in silence

I just say Thank you

Amen

Part V

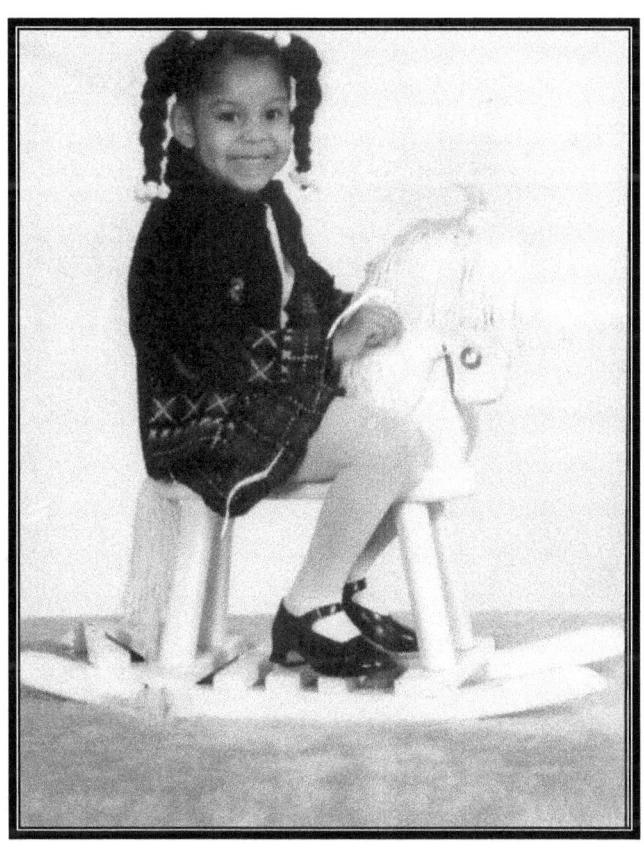

Lesson 5

If you feel the need to boast, boast about the sacrifice that he made for us. Boast about the cross, his goodness, his mercy, and his grace. Boast about the love of Jesus Christ. He could have picked anyone else but he chose us and we should all be thankful because it could have been another way. Everything that has breath should be praising his name…JESUS!

Walston

3 a.m.

So I tiptoe through the hush
Only to hear the snores and whimpers of rest
Through the front door to enter the heavens of the outside
I sit upon my porch, and I adore God

I listen to the winds blow a breeze
Capturing the essence of the harmonies
Of creation
And beauty of pure existence

I watch as the crickets hop along
Into the dewy grass
As spiders cast their web
To create safe havens for their young
And capture their prey

The trucks blew horns from the distant highway
As the trains, friction causes an eruption on the tracks
The illumination of the street light
Cast a shadow of my silhouette
Hovering over me, from my wooden panes

The oak tree bows
To the pine in salutations
While the grass admires the
Flowers hues in an appreciation of their bloom

The North Star shines bright
As the Orion converses with the big, and little dippers
As they admire the crevices of the moon
Waiting patiently for the sun to rise
and state her claim on a new day

I close my eyes
And hear
The whispers of this phenomenon
Called nature

Acceding my head in prayer
I hoist my hands with praise
For I am overwhelmed by
His conception

I am enthralled with his omnipotence
Engaged in his substance
Muted by his glory
As I sit upon my porch and adore God

Daily Prayer XIII

I jump, kick, and scream at the top of my lungs
This is the day that the Lord has made!
I will rejoice and be glad in it!
For this day is never duplicated
It is a day of accomplishment, and completion
It is a day to honor the metamorphosing
Of my spirit

I delight in your joy
I honor your sacrifice
For I promise to make the best of everyday you wish to provide
God,
My gratitude cannot be spoken of
For I, you're humble
Servant will kneel at you every command
Amen

Do You Know what Praise is?

You can't deny his work
You can't forget what he has done
Yet you sit there as if he has done nothing
You hear the good word
You are a witness to the truth
But your body is limp
And you seem unconcerned with his mercy
You are silent
And you know just yesterday
You were calling his name
And he answered your prayers

How selfish
How indignant
How shameful
Is your lack of acknowledgment

He is the Lord our God
He makes a way out of no way
He is a lawyer in a courtroom
A doctor who can heal
He gives us life and resolves all issues
He doesn't just do it for me
He does it for you

And if you can't shout Hallelujah
Just for breathing another day
Getting another chance
Never duplicating the day
And teaching you that he is great
Then you don't know what praise is

Daily Prayer XIV

No doubt
No death
No worries
No wicked
No pain
No poverty
No affliction
No agitation
No tragedy
No Terror
No ignorance
No Insult
No chaos
No confusion
No clutter
No condemnation
No complacency
No complications
Hey SATAN!
When I see JESUS
I will sing and shout the victory!

They saw heaven

Beaming through sky
He stretched his hand out
As they walked to the light
The clouds magnificent full with the moisture of mercy
The saints were gathered around
Awaiting for the announcement
And their names to be called

To the Little Girl Who Loved to Dance

They smiled
As joy filled
Their souls
The angels strum
The harmonies of praise
And the streets were paved with gold
The mansions were in full view
And the milk and honey flowed through the rivers of life
There was no crying
No sadness
Only tears of joy

Hallelujah they sang
Hallelujah they praised

For they knew the moment had arrived
They had repented
They had been dipped in the fountain
They had accepted his name
And the Holy Ghost ran through their veins
They were reborn

Hallelujah they sang
Hallelujah they praised

For heaven was amidst
What a glorious day
For all the saints prayed in thanks
When they saw
Heaven

Daily Prayer XV

See Lord, today I can't find a trendy way
To express
I want to express to you the certainty
Of keeping you in my life
I don't know anything else to say
Other than

It would never be in my interest to serve anyone but
you
I know there are times when I doubt myself
But because you know the outcome
You still keep me in your site
Even when I am not worthy Lord

You don't look at the layers of disappointment
Your extension of forgiveness draws me to shame, if I
harm my fellow brother
It is not in my best interest to yield to temptation and
forget the promises I made to you
I am almost certain that a catastrophe would take
place if I ever denied you
I could lose weight, friends, and all my possession
But God, I can't lose you
I tried it my way and it didn't work

So Lord I beg of you never let me go
For I am certain that you are my Lord
For I am certain that you are always by my side
Please never leave
Me Lord

To the Little Girl Who Loved to Dance

Part VI

Lesson 6

Rebuke all negativity in your life because you are one of God's greatest treasures. You only have a place for joy and happiness in your spirit. Nothing should ever hold you down for the God we serve believes in his people being uplifted at all times! Now you know Satan can never when, Praise God in advance!

Walston

Restore my family

We didn't choose them
We can't hold hate
Even in dysfunction
Our love should never dissipate

There should always be unity
Not just because we are genetically disposed
But because we are a family
Even if we don't sometimes know

There will be disagreements
And misunderstandings
But as long as there is a God
We will all have safe landings

So let's not cry or fret any more
We can look to the hills
For him to restore

Daily Prayer XVI

Dear God
All of this negativity surrounds me
I am in the midst of a battle that I can't win
I am at my wits in, and don't know how to focus or pray
I would pray for strength but no longer do I want to be strong
I need a release
I need some comfort
I need some safety in your arms

I want you to hold my hand
I want you to place
Peace back in my spirit
I want you to speak to me and tell me everything will be ok
I want you to reassure me of your presence
And remove Satan from his comfort
I need you
Dear Lord
I ask for a release if only for a moment
I need to smile

There is no doubt

There is sometimes love
Sometime fear
There is sometimes dismay
But I know you are always here

There is sometimes good
There is sometimes bad
But even in my glum
I can never be sad

There is sometimes anger
There is sometimes rain
I know that the storm will pass
And I shall feel no more pain

There is sometimes confusion
There is sometimes chaos
So I read and meditate on your word
So I can never be lost

There are all these feelings
But I never allow them to consume or put me out
Because it is you that I trust dear God, so rest assured
that there is no doubt

Daily Prayer XVII

God if I had a dime for every time I claimed I would
change
I would be rich
And it is sad to say
That I defeat and fight myself

I know what I am supposed to do
And what I should be doing
But I find myself caught up in this world
Which has no place for me

I am aware you can't serve two Gods
And my flesh is winning my battle everyday
Therefore, I am asking you to forgive me
Because my spirit knows better, but my flesh is weak
My intentions are good
However, my actions are contradictions

I know I do not deserve your love
Moreover, the sacrifices you have made
Nevertheless, I am asking that you be patient with me
I do not want you to harden my heart
I want to make a change
I want to do right
So Lord,
Please help me
Just do not let me go

I know that through Christ all things are possible
And if I am wrong to ask this of you God
I am sorry
However, I know not what to do

If it had not been

Where would I be if Eve and Adam were not cast out of the Garden of Eden?

And if God did not decide to flood the world and put Noah on that ark

If Abraham didn't obey God

If Jacob had not fathered Joseph

If Pharaoh had not held them captive in Egypt

If Moses did not climb, mount Sinai

If they didn't find the promise land

And David did not write the Psalms

If Mary didn't obey the Gabriel and opted out of her responsibility

If God did not sent his only son
Who would die for all of my sins, and iniquities?

Someone tell me

Where would I be?

Daily Prayer XVIII

Dear God as a child of yours
I understand why I am scorned
I understand my reaping
And I understand my duties

Just like a child
I am hard headed
Sometimes disobedient
And unfortunately disrespectful

Just like I child
I hear you
And don't always listen
I know your power
Nevertheless, I try you, time and time again

Just like a child
I get ashamed when I disappoint you
And hope that you hold no ill will
I try to please you when I can
Just so, you don't push me away

Nevertheless, just like a child
Because of my foundation
I have received the necessary lessons to make
informed decisions
Just like a child,
deep inside we find out later in life that our parents
will not lead us astray

I know you have never placed anything in my heart
that is malice

I know you convict me when I need to make decisions
I know you show me signs so that I am aware

As a child, I say thank you father
for being a good parent
Thank you for not giving up on me yet.

To the Little Girl Who Loved to Dance

Part VII

Lesson 7

We pay for so much in this world. Did you know it cost nothing to praise? That is because Jesus already paid the price for us. Take your hands off your wallets and purses and just stop and give God some earnest and much deserved praise. He keeps on blessing you and that is all he asks. It does not cost a thing to say, THANK YOU JESUS

Walston

Daily Prayer XIX

Lord when I forget
You don't
When I want to quit
You will not let me
When I want to wallow in self-pity
You place me safely in your arms

When I want to make the wrong decision
You give me a choice

When I do not understand
You explain

When I do not believe
You teach me

When my heart is heavy
You release me from the pain

When I cry
You wipe my tears

When I need something unconditional
You always love me

Lord thank you

Because you always just do

Does it really matter?

All of the hell you caused in your early years
The beers you drank
The drugs you used
The hurtful words you have said
The lies you told
The hearts you broke
The friends you neglected
The people you tricked
The money you spent
The materials you owned
The times you skipped service
The good word you avoided

Does it really matter?
No,
Because what are you doing now?
If you have repented, and accepted Jesus as you Lord and savior
Know that this is a new day
And that was yesterday

Therefore, it only matters if you still serve the world and not God

Daily Prayer XX

Lord,
It is so funny
Your work
Your love
Your word
And your truth
It is so simple
However, people find it difficult
To follow you
And your doctrine
I am not sure why
This world is tempting with all of it glitz and glamour
The money, the status, the fame
However, what people do not understand is that the things of this world are temporary
But the treasure of you is eternal
So Lord,
Today I pray
That we all understand your worth
Because there is nobody greater than you

Beautiful

Oh how glorious
Oh how wondrous
Oh how perfect
Oh how great
Oh how loving
Oh how soothing
Oh how joyful
Oh how blissful

Oh how beautiful you are
For you are an angel created and molded by the
loving hand of God

Daily Prayer XXI

In my closet
I find a secret place
To unfold the dark feelings
To share my thoughts
To bellow out my emotions
To plea and beg for forgiveness

I find the time to pray
And ask you to cover my family
To remove iniquity
To free us from the bondage of our minds
To open our heart

I find the time to ask you
For forgiveness
To free me from myself
To enlighten me, strengthen my knowledge, and
wisdom

I find the time to pray for my friends, and my enemies
That they have opened there heart, and accepted you
That they know who you are
And put their trust in you, and only you

In my closet, I take the time
To separate myself from this world
And give you my
Time and attention

To the Little Girl Who Loved to Dance

Because there is power in prayer
And I know you are listening

To the Little Girl Who Loved to Dance

Part VIII

Walston

Lesson 8

Love should always come first. Embrace it and hold it in the utmost regard. Find comfort in love, and adore loves essence. Allow your soul to consume it daily. Permit your mind to find loves peace. This way hate can find no place to reside in your heart.

Walston

We can smile together

We can
If we did not abhor each other

We can
If we hold each other

We can
If we told each other daily, I love you

We can
If we forgot about the past and focused on the future

We can
If we embrace God's wonders

We can
If we attend to his word

We can
If we sacrifice and submit

We can
If we could see beyond the physical

If we honor each other as brothers and sisters and understand, we are all connected to each other by his omnipotence
Then we can smile together

Daily Prayer XXII

Dear God
I feel a smile in my spirit

Because today was yet another day that you gave me
a chance to prove myself to you

You know my worth,
You know my heart, and I know you have my best
interest

I know that I could never be perfect as you
However, I thank God; you made me in your image

I know your perfection, and I would hope to one day
to be a third of what you have made me to be
I love you

And my heart is filled with joy
Because you never leave me, and honor your word in
truth

So Lord
I am happy because you are who you say you are
And have never failed me yet

A Heavy Heart

I cannot
Sleep
Eat
Think

To the Little Girl Who Loved to Dance

Breath
And worst of all
I cannot pray

My mind is heavy
My thoughts are cloudy
And I cannot see
Well
Clearly

You see my heart is
Full of pain
Misunderstanding
And I just don't
Know
What or how
When or where

I want to close my eyes
And blink into a new place
Change my name
Or at least the color
Of my soul
Because it is blue

I cannot cry
And I am weeping
Wondering if I am reaping
A fruitful seed that I did not sow
I do not know

However, I cannot sleep
Eat
Think or breathe
And worst of all

I cannot pray
Because my heart is heavy

Daily Prayer XXIII

Dear God there is so much injustice
there is so much hate in this world
Nevertheless, I cannot be weary of this
All I can do is pray for those that do not have an understanding

All I can do is pray that we as a nation somehow find peace
I have read your words and I know that history repeats itself
Even if it is not on the same ground, in the same place, at the same time

I should never be shocked
Lord, I still long to see your glory, and I witness your goodness every day
I will not fret because nothing in this world is under Satan's control

It is only you who can commanded the sea to part and open the skies to produce rain
I know it is you who brings sunrays and make the birds chirp

Therefore, I have to believe that all of your intentions are good and this is your handy work
However, I also know that I have to continue to pray

To the Little Girl Who Loved to Dance

In my prayers, I must continuously praise you
because you are omnipotent
You are merciful, you are grace, and you are love,
because you are God.

Respectfully yours

I do not praise you
Because you are not God

And I cannot worship you
Because praising you would be

Well not rewarded

And I cannot hold you or uplift you
Because I don't have it in me

I do not trust you because you are a liar

You cannot be my comforter because you make me
uncomfortable

I cannot submit to you because my spirit desires more
You cannot trick me because I have learned my
lesson

You do not bless me because you don't hold blessings
You can have the materials because he has a better
plan

And nothing
He has given me can land in your hands

I cannot offer you love, and you do not have much more

So Satan

I am rebuking you in the name of Jesus

Respectfully yours

Daily Prayer XXIV

Lord

You know

And I don't

But I trust

Only you

Lord you know

That I can't serve

No one so true

Lord

You hold

My life in your hand

To the Little Girl Who Loved to Dance

When I am lost and in doubt

I just know how to stand

Lord

I know you

Won't let me down
And in the event of my mishaps

Please chastise me

But stay around

Lord

For I need

Only you

Because Lord daily I need to be renewed

Walston

To the Little Girl Who Loved to Dance

Part IX

Walston

Lesson 9

Do not always be impressed by a person's appearance or how their articulate words. They can be deceitful. Pay attentions to their activity and their actions because at some point their true self will appear. Remember Satan was one of God's most charming and cunning angels and look where he landed. Right out of the kingdom!

You decide

I can say he tricked me
But you gave me a choice

And it is not he
Who will be judged
On judgment day
It will be my actions
And obedience which will lead my way

So if I listen, and fall prey
Because my flesh is weak
It will be no one's fault because it is you I should always seek

Pointing fingers and blaming others
For my own strife
At the end of the day will not save my life

I must always be self-aware
And no that my God is able
And it is he who cares

If I stay stern in my faith, and focus on your word
He will never have a hold on my life
Because it is God, I am supposed to serve

Daily Prayer XXV

Dear God
It is evident that not everyone holds good intentions,

I understand that some people may have hidden agendas,

But Lord, I know I cannot have concern
For other peoples tactics and agendas
I cannot concern myself with how people choose to live their lives
I can only be concerned with mine

Nevertheless, Lord, I would be lying if I told you it did not bother me
Sometimes I find myself caught up in the middle of the things that I question
And to be honest I don't know what to do
But it is not my place

Lord, I am asking you to remove any feelings of unbalance
Any feelings of concern that I have for matters that are not mine
I just ask you Lord to deal with those that do
Also, deal with me, if I hold any haste in my heart
If I treat people unfairly
If I am unkind and don't extend

Lord I do not want anything to interfere with my salvation
I know mistakes are inevitable
But Lord,
I want to make sure that I do all I know how to do
And as long as it is pleasing to you

Then Lord, I will be satisfied

A breath of fresh air

It is the breeze that blows the wind in my lungs
The exchange and speech of the unknowing tongue

It is the freedom, which has wrestled with my flesh
And the sound of the angels who hear my harmony

It is the night, which I find my comfort, and forget my fear

It is the sun, which beams on my face, letting me know a new day is here

It is the door that opens when I release the stress
And the so called coincidences, which verify I am blessed

It is the prayer that holds the word, unspoken
Because God knows my heart, and reminds me, I am chosen

It is the conviction, which allows me
To be better than I use to be

It is the consciousness that makes me self-aware
It is knowing that God still loves me
For he is my
Breath of fresh air

Daily Prayer XXVI

Dear Lord,
I sometimes don't understand why others don't see what I see

I have seen your handy work ever since I decided that this was a part of my destiny
Then I remember not so long ago
When I was stubborn and refused to submit to your word

I thought that this world had more to offer, and I still wanted you in my back pocket

I did not want you to leave me but I wanted to try anything Satan offered me

However, I did not realize I made life so much more difficult for myself
And after falling far enough where I thought I couldn't reach you

You dropped your hand down and pulled me up
You did not ask me any questions, you just required me to accept you

So that you could save me from myself

And yes each day after was a challenge but was the best decision I ever made

No, I never became perfect
Nevertheless, I was willing to try a little more every day

To the Little Girl Who Loved to Dance

Until I understood, my life was in your hands

And each and every day thereafter although a process
I realized they were a part of my progress

So Lord,
I sometimes do not understand why others do not see
what I see

That is ok
Because I have to focus on bettering me and pray for
those who are making the same decisions

As I once did before
The nice thing is that I now know it is you, always
opening a door

We all have to make a decision and I just hope
Others decide to follow you

Make a choice

Take him for granted
Hide from your truth
Tell him a lie
And expect no fruit

Pretend it did not happen
Act as if it does not matter
And if you're left in the valley
Your life will surely shatter

Change your position

Find a new mission
Repent to the Lord and
You will be forgiven

Call on his name
Trust in his hand
Turn your life over to Christ
Just make a stand

Daily Prayer XXVII

Dear Lord,
I thank you heavenly father
For all you have done
and what you do
because I know there is nothing in this world
that you don't touch
that you don't control.

I smile in the morning
Because it is you who wakes me
It is you who gives me breath, and it is you who gives me life

And for whatever reason
you decided
I was going to have another chance and be blessed another day

And sometimes I feel as if I do not know,
I don't know how, but at the end
you show me and make me realize the truth

So Lord,

To the Little Girl Who Loved to Dance

I am grateful that you love me
and you chose me to be better than I was yesterday

So today Lord,
I praise you, and thank you
because you change my life each minute
because each day I get to serve you
I know I am only getting closer to the kingdom

Amen

To the Little Girl Who Loved to Dance

Part X

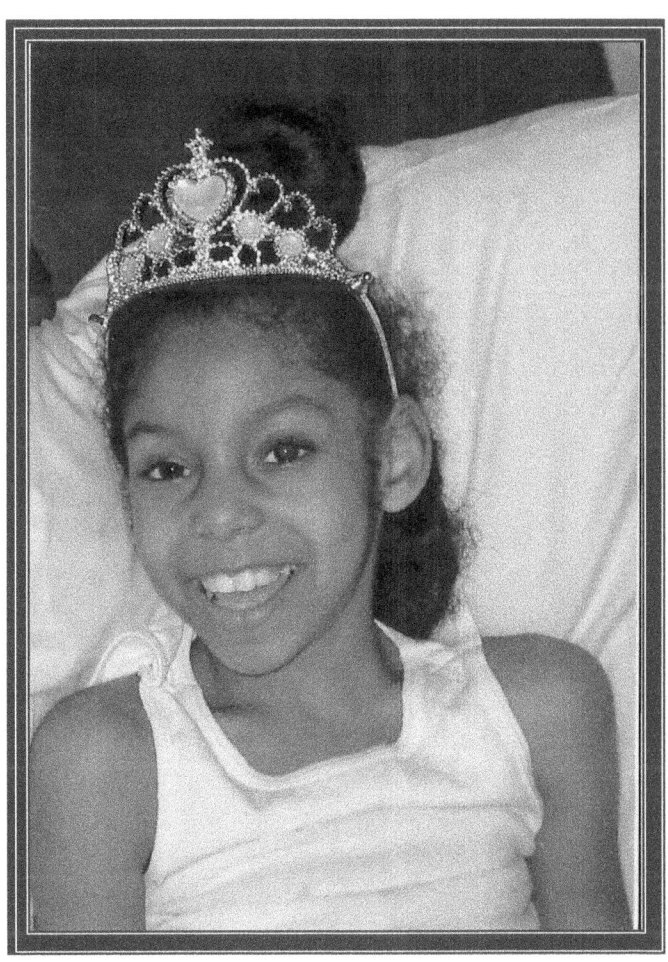

Lesson 10

When you are blessed, make sure you are also blessing the next person. A chain reaction should occur when you are provided with your needs. Do not hoard your blessings, there are others out there waiting for theirs and you may be the person God has ordered to assist the next man. If you do not, your blessings may be shortened or blocked.

Walston

Contract

You gave to me
And I am going to give it back
You set me free
When I was under attack

You showed me
There was a better way
Each day gets better
And I refuse to stray

You gave me hope
You kept me still
In my process
I learn that it is all in your will

I'm running each race
And focusing on each test
I am reading your word
And I am no longer restless

You make me smile
Even in the rain
And as long as I follow you
There will be no more pain

I won't give up
Because you never gave up on me
I am going keep going forward
And promise never to flee

Daily Prayer XXVIII

Dear God,
Life is so precious
We must not forget the importance of living
Because we don't have a life time on this earth

But we

Can have an eternity in your kingdom
Our time here must be spent wisely
Because no one knows when
They will breath their last breathe

Therefore, we must do what is necessary
When we are faced with life's test
Lord, life is so precious and we sometimes forget
We squander away precious time
Concerned with worry fear and doubt

We walk around aimlessly with no focus and no
particular route

We must
Be conscious before our time is up
because
Once we close our eyes, our time has ended
So we must never forget
and have no regrets

We must put you first, even in the worst
because we have crossed over
we want to be in the number
of those who sit at your right hand

To the Little Girl Who Loved to Dance

How did you decide?

The colors of the rainbow

Better yet, color

How did you decide who was going to give birth and be a mother?

How did you decide that it would only take you 7 days?

How did you decide to make all of the creatures that you created?

How did you decide what belonged in the sea?

In the mountains and the desert and in all the skies we see

How did you decide what fruit would set us free?

Why did you give us free will?

And that infamous tree

Why does the water cover most of the land?

How did the serpent have the ability?

To trick your creation called man

How did you decide his name?

And a partner to complete

I wonder if it ever angered you that in temptation they became weak

Daily Prayer XXIX

Lord,
Did I do good today?
Did I honor your word?
Did I pray?
Did I call on your name?
Did I praise?
Did I thank you for all of these wonderful days?

Lord,
Did I share my testimony?
Did I tell them your life stories?
Did I live selflessly?
Or just for me

Lord,
Did I extend love?
Smile instead of frown
Or was I silent
And did not utter a sound

Lord,
Did I please you?
Was I obedient to your word?
Or did I ignore what you have done in my life?
I hope not, that would be absurd

Lord,
Did I say thank you?

To the Little Girl Who Loved to Dance

Because you gave me another chance today
And I will praise you in advance
And I promise not to stray

There are not enough things to say
And I feel I am always
Asking
You have done so much in my life
And I feel as if time is passing

All I need you to do
I think of your goodness and what you have done

However, I cannot articulate
The way I feel
Or what I want to say

But dear Lord,
I want you to know that I am thankful to you each day
And although I cannot produce wind, rain, and spew fire from my mouth
My heart is pure, very sure that I am grateful and secure
So Lord,
Just know that I do thank you for each and everyday
Just know I will continue
And will always remember regardless of my works
I will stop and pray

Daily Prayer XXX (for the Evening)

Dear Lord
I say good Night

As
I empty the troubles of yesterday
Into the bowl of obsolete

I hold my hand out to you and
Thank you for
Peace of mind

I am glad for the lessons presented
So that my knowledge can increase
And assist in my guidance

Continue to mold me Lord
Place in order the necessities
Of your desires for me
Just to hold onto the
Hem of your garment
Is more than enough payment
So I say again to you
Oh wonderful father
Thank you for the evening
And I thank you for the beginning
Soon to start again at sunrise

To the little girl who loved to dance

To the little girl that loved to dance

And wave her hands above the clouds

To feel free and apart of the heavens

While they salute God

And whistle to the melodies

To little girl who loved to dance

Hold in her spirits the joys of now

While releasing the pain of the icky world

And embracing the blessing of who he is and how

To the little girl who loved to dance

Stand proud

And respect the bow of the trees

And see peace as it sits still

To little girl who loved to dance

Who received her halo and wings

And understands that her journey was God will

Epilogue

Diamond Coren Brown was diagnosed with Huntington Disease at the age of seven. Huntington Disease is a rare disease that is genetically passed. Most individuals that have been diagnosed with the disease range between the ages of 20 and 50 years old. When this disease is diagnosed in a child, the progression is more rapid than that of an adult. Huntington Disease is a terminal disease in which the nerve cells in the brain deteriorate causing an uncontrollable jerking of the body. Currently, there is no cure for this disease. Once the disease has affected the nervous system, the symptoms can only be managed, but are not curable.

On February 16, 2011, Diamond lost her battle with the disease. As devastating as the lost was, all who knew Diamond knew how much she had suffered. No one will ever know why God took her so early in life, but those who understand God's perfect work, know she is in a better place. Diamond is no longer suffering at the behest of Huntington Disease. She is now smiling in the heavens. She will be remembered for the joy, and love she brought to those who knew her.

It is important for people to be aware of this illness, and make sure they further educate themselves. Awareness is the key component when trying to fight this battle. Parents must be aware of their medical history, as well as, the history of their spouses and companions. Although knowing and understanding potential medical history may not prevent illness to occur; it can prepare individuals for the stages that may transpire.

Diamond is, and was loved. All who had the privilege of meeting her loved her. I knew her as, *The little Girl who loved to Dance*. She also loved to sing and play. She kept a permanent smile on her face.

Diamond Coren Brown, I dedicate, and honor you with, "The Little Girl who loved to Dance." May God continue to watch over you, and keep you safely in his loving arms.

Acknowledgments

I cannot begin to thank any one unless I first give honor to God. In everything I touch, in everything I write, he is present. He keeps me motivated to focus on my true purpose.

I would also like to thank Charity Brown the mother of the late Diamond Brown for allowing me to create this book in honor and memory of this beautiful child. I would like to thank my mother for pushing me to complete this project, even when I didn't know how I was going to do it. In addition, I would like to thank Shakeya Bradshaw for all of her hard work and patience. Reginald Conyard, for his time and attention to detail. I would like to thank those who take the time out to read my work and provide me feedback. Without their attention, this project would not be complete. Finally, I would like to thank everyone who believed in me even when I didn't believe in myself. Your support helped me make it through. You know who you are, and I extend many blessings and much love.

About the Author

Anica Walston is a native of Petersburg, VA. This is first of two poetry books, which have been published in 2011. The other is entitled, "Yes, I am Woman," a poetry book written for women. Anica recently published her first novel entitled, Generational Dysfunctions Vol. I," and is currently working on the sequel.

Anica created, "Respect the Gender," which is centered on being of service to the women in her community, and publishing her work. She is currently working on her Master's in Counseling Studies at Capella University (2013). Anica loves to write, and has a great desire to work with others on their visions. Her faith is stern, and she believes as long as she is obedient and focused that God will order her steps.

All of Anica's poetry, books, and novels are available on Amazom.com as well as her Respect the Gender Website.

http://www.wix.com/anicawalston/rtg

www.ingramcontent.com/pod-product-compliance
Lightning Source LLC
Chambersburg PA
CBHW070500100426
42743CB00010B/1703